beautiful
TENERIFE

DISTRIBUTOR: **GARCIA Y CORREA**
DISTRIBUIDORA EDITORIAL CANARIA
Quevedo, 3 - La Salle, 9
Teléfonos: 22 98 40 - 41 - 42
22 96 46 - 47

TEXT: **GILBERTO ALEMAN**
DESIGN AND ILLUSTRATIONS: **RAFAEL GURREA**
CO-ORDINATOR: **OCTAVIO CASTRO**
PHOTOS ARCHIVES: **LITO A. ROMERO, S. A.**

PRINTED BY LITOGRAFIA A. ROMERO, S. A.
SANTA CRUZ DE TENERIFE. (SPAIN)
ISBN 84 300 6009 X
DEPOSITO LEGAL. TF. 1.418 - 1972

PARTIAL VIEW OF SANTA CRUZ

The City of Santa Cruz de Tenerife is a symphony in white and blue — the colours of its harbour ensign. Due to its fine harbour it is one of the most important ports of the Canary Islands. It owes its very heavy traffic to the fact that fishing boats and ships from all over the world call there. At present a mole is under construction to ensure still further development.

1

PLAZA DE ESPAÑA

Due to the heavy traffic of its harbour, Santa Cruz de Tenerife has at all times been mainly a commercial city where goods from all over the world can be purchased. Nevertheless, it must not be forgotten that one of the main industries of the island has today become the development of tourism, and that this industry now complements the fishing business that was once predominant.

The growth of the capital has in the past few years surpassed every expectation. In 1940, the population consisted of only some 60,000 inhabitants; today the capital has a population of more than 200,000. This increase is due partly to normal growth, but also to the steady migration of people from surrounding villages, who flock to the city where more and better paid job are to be found. As a consequence, the authorities are faced with various new problems, mainly fast planning and building in order to avoid an acute shortage of living accommodation.

The city is a city of white houses, the vast residential quarters with their iridescent gardens throwing patches of colour amongst the dazzling white. These residential quarters contrast vividly with the dynamic intensity of the commercial and administrative centres.

Santa Cruz prides itself on its many beautiful squares, all representing a peaceful oasis to the lingering passer-by. Take for example the Plaza de España at the entrance to the city, or, higher up, the Candelaria Square with it's beautiful central monument representing the Virgin of Candelaria, carved in white marble by the Italian sculptor Canova. Also the Plaza del Príncipe, striking because of its romantic aura, which was once a convent garden. Ascending the Calle de Castillo, the main business street of the city, we reach the Weile Square with its marble fountain and its glossy laurel trees. The Plaza de los Patos seems almost Andalusian with its flaming mosaics and it's bubbling fountains. Still another square worth mentioning is the one of the Hospital Militar, attractive principally because of its Indian Laurel trees, a beautiful old species with ivy climbing about it's thick trunks. The Indian laurel is found scattered across the whole island, but it was originally imported from Cuba. Addi-

PANORAMIC VIEW OF SANTA CRUZ

3

PUERTO DE SANTA CRUZ

tional to these well-known Plazas, we have smaller and nameless squares all over the city: little green squares, alight with all shades of green in the golden sunset.

The main green zone of the city, however, is the beautiful Municipal Park — an enchanting exotic park in the very heart of the city, with charming paths amidst lush vegetation where practically every species of sub-tropical plants is to be found.

PLAYA OF ALMACIGA

5

PUNTA DEL HIDALGO

The city has but few historical monuments. The Palacio de Carta on Candelaria Square is one of them, but although it has been restored, the old manorial building has been turned into a bank. The church of Iglesia de la Concepción is of both architectural and historical interest; in this church are kept relics and historical trophies, such as the flags captured by our people from the English Admiral Nelson.

The history of the Canaries is comparatively modern, considering that the Archipelago was only annexed to the Crown of Castile in the year 1496. Until then the islands were inhabited by the aborigines called Guanches, a noble and proud race of undefined origin. It was don Alonso Fernández de Lugo who finally conquered Tenerife and subdued the Guanches. He disembarked at the island on the day of the Holy Cross; hence the name of Santa Cruz de Tenerife. This was towards the end of the 15th century, and in consequence the capital of Santa Cruz de Tenerife has not yet much of a history; in fact, it is more towards the interior of the island that we come across more important historical places that bear witness to the war between the Guanches and the Spaniards.

Today, Santa Cruz has developed into a modern city with modern stores — and a yong, modern generation is gradually replacing the past generations of fishermen. Santa Cruz is a progressive city whose former rural aspect has changed into a modern skyline. Pioneers and developers of the city are faced with new problems, for they must build today what will become the city of tomorrow.

Along the coastline of Santa Cruz de Tenerife we find charming and delightful corners, like Almaciga, situated beyond San Andrés. It is a fishing harbour and has a small beach where tourists often bask in the sun. A conglomeration of white houses on the fringe of the rocky Anaga range, where the land extends in the form of small islands right into the deep blue sea.

VIEW FROM LAS MERCEDES ON THE TEIDE

But let us leave behind us the progressive city of the Adelantados and turn towards one splendid spot embedded among the mountains. It was in this place that there one lived the «poor Hidalgo», a Guanche king whose name has become legendary; the place is therefore called Punta de Hidalgo in his honour. Formerly an arid land, inhabited only by fisherman, this place is gradually developing into a centre of relaxation of tired businessmen and people who wish to escape the noise of larger communities. Efforts have also been made in the agricultural direction and we find quite a few banana plantations here, like everywhere else on the island, for the Canarian bananas are exported in vast quantities to markets abroad.

PARTIAL VIEW OF BAJAMAR

NATURAL SWIMMING POOLS AT BAJAMAR

The coastline is black and austere, yet sometimes a softer scenery catches the eye of the visitor, such as a tiny beach, or a hidden little bay, where fishermen whose boats have crossed the seas for endless months relax for a short while. In Punta de Hidalgo the sun shines down in all its fullness, so that even the gigantic volcano Teide, which dominates the archipelago from the centre of the island, looks merely like a vague and gentle vision in the far distance.

This rugged route does not exclude the presence of small gardens, even though these resemble more a jungle of species and colours. Nothing is planned in these gardens, everything grows wild and naturally.

A profusion of vividly tinted flowers overflow the white walls of the farm houses, a riot of iridescent hues.

Nature is generous on this island, as is evident in the variety of it's vegetation and the lush richness of it's shades and

colours. The natives strive to plant more trees along the roadsides, and these trees will, in this ideal climate, reproduce naturally. Green trees contrasting with the striking red of the poinsettias; a charming and restful sight for every visitor.

The islander loves nature. He respects the trees and strives day by day to enrich the earth he has inherited from his ancestors, this earth that is blessed with a climate which allows the miracle of flowers growing permanently all the year round on the Isle of Eternal Spring.

The landscape is serene, trees serving

as a frame to the picture of the majestic Teide, whose eternal presence dominates the island. Yes, serenity is the only true word to express the peaceful atmosphere that exists in this quiet spot at the foot of the Mercedes mountains. Here we find ourselves amongst dense forests of glossy laurels and Canary pines.

The land is fertile, rich in vegetation and a striking contrast to some dry and barren zones of the island, where erupting volcanoes have turned the soil sterile, and where traces of the flow of hot lava still exist. The vast and devastated zones bear witness to the tragedy of a tormented earth.

The silence of this place at the foot of Monte Mercedes, far from the noise and bustle of urban areas, makes it an ideal spot for relaxation and contemplation. It is one of the most peaceful spots on the island, this little place situated almost next to the house where lived the great musician Teobaldo Power, composer of the «Cantos Canarios».

CHURCH OF SANTO CRISTO DE LA LAGUNA

PANORAMA IN MESA DEL MAR

13

Bajamar stretches along a black beach where submerged reefs form a natural swimming pool. For this reason it has already, in the years past, been «discovered» by many holidaymakers. Of late it has developed very quickly into a centre for water sports fans. Supported by tourist industry,

Bajamar is gradually developing into an important holiday resort to which visitors from all over the world are coming.

Together with Punta del Hidalgo, Bajamar has unlimited potentialities for further tourist development. New hotels, apartments, restaurants and shops are springing

MESA DEL MAR

up, thus offering the visitor more than just the recreational facilities of underwater fishing and other squatic sports.

From the insignificant little rural locality it once was, Bajamar has in the past ten years developed into an important beach resort, visited on week-ends and during high season by large numbers of tourists and local holidaymakers.

Built on a lagoon, surrounded by mountains, San Cristóbal de La Laguna was first and former capital of the Canarian Archipelago. Its straight old streets testify to its history, that goes back to the first years

MESA DEL MAR

CAMPO DE LA VICTORIA AND TEIDE

of the Spanish conquest. The Adelantados supreme authorities of the Archipelago) used to live in Cristóbal de La Laguna. Today it is the seat of the University of the Canaries.

La Laguna used to be the main political, religious, military and cultural centre. This town is really steeped in history, and most art treasures of importance are to be seen here.

The town is situated in the midst of the beautiful and fertile Valley of Aguerra, but more and more land has to be surrendered to the necessity of urbanizations, and to the extention of the city. Authorities, however, strive to preserve nature, and beautiful old trees still border the ancient agricultural zone, even though it has turned into a residential centre. The singular beauty of this old town in the midst of this valley, is the striking contrast between rural

NORTH COAST

NORTH COAST

and urban scenes, between the plains and the mountains, between yesterday and today.

Ancient convents are set off perfectly against the background of the historical town of San Cristóbal de La Laguna. With their carved wooden balconies, they are characteristic of typical Canarian architecture, still to be found in many other communities.

Four important celebrations take place every year in La Laguna. One is the Semana Santa, or Passion Week, and is of traditional character: typical is the procession where life-size statues of the Saints are carried aloft through the streets. Another festivity is the one of Corpus Christi, on which day elaborate scented flower carpets, combined with much love, skill and patience, adorn the main squares and streets. The celebration of San Benito resembles

more an annual parish fair, enlivened by the climax of importants folklore demonstrations. And finally, we have the festival of the Cristo de La Laguna, on which day people gather by thousands around the image of the Cristo; it is moreover the occasion for a succession of cultural, religious, and popular events that take place in the month of September.

Tacoronte overlooks the sea. You may choose whatever point of the parish you like, and it will always offer you a glimpse of the ocean.

Tacoronte was one of the pioneer cities for Tourist Development on Tenerife, and continues to be strongly interested in the further development of this industry. In Mesa del Mar important hotel buildings have been erected along the rocky coastline.

FLOWERS AND FOLKLORE

Close to the sea, modern buildings have sprung up and contrast vividly with the rural farmhouses and native shops on the upper hill slopes, where farmers mainly cultivate the vine.

This part of the island is proof of the triumph of man over the craggy mountainous land. Streets have been built from all points that lead direct to the sea.

Tacoronte overlooks the sea from any angle, from its mountain peaks, its green fields, its peaceful roads bordered by acacias — and even from those old farmhouses up on the hill which look like silent reminders of peace and work.

The alternating landscape of the northern part of the island has no counterpart elsewhere in the world. From the top of the mountains down to the blue sea the landscape stands out in an extraordinary gradation of green hues: from the dark green shades of pine forests and cypresses down to the lighter green of farmland and banana plantations. Yet, generous and fertile as the earth may be in this region, it is nevertheless a landscape that was not created by nature alone. It is man who has given final form to the scenery.

CARNATION FIELDS

Year after year, with the quiet equanimity so typical of the Canarian, he has gradually given his surroundings a definite shape. He built roads up into the mountains, overcoming the difficulties this enterprise offered; he invented new ways of cultivating terrace-like fields on the steep slopes and built stone walls to protect his crop from the winds; he bored galleries deep into the interior of the earth in order to obtain the water that is so precious and rare on this island.

Miles and miles of water galleries were bored and networks of pipe lines installed in order that the life-giving water might be obtained for the irrigation of fields, gardens and plantations everywhere. For this reason we speak of this northern scenery as being truly the result of man's labour, proof of his creative spirit and his tireless activity. Much hardship did he take upon himself. In many places it was, for example, necessary to transport fertile earth from one part of the island to another that was rocky and barren. But never did the islander relax his efforts to turn even barren soil fertile, and it is thanks to his incessant activity that agriculture has prospered and developed successfully.

VALLEY OF OROTAVA

The success of some products varied with the years. At first it was the wine that was exported in great quantity, for the Malvasian grapes had reached almost universal fame and were the main economical basis for the farmer. This was followed by the boom in Cochineal, used for the manufacture of tints and lipsticks. Next came the sugar cane — and today it is the banana plant which reigns supreme, together with the cultivation of tomatoes and potatoes.

Anxious to improve living conditions, the farmers of the island are seeking new ways and possibilities to make the best use of their land and the climate it is blessed with. As a result we have today a vast variety of agricultural products, from all kinds of fruit to a wide choice of flowers, from products grown in greenhouses to the recently successfully grown strawberries.

TOWN OF OROTAVA

PREPARING THE CARPETS FOR CORPUS

OCTAVA CORPUS CHRISTI

AND FINAL RESULT OF THIS GREAT ART

CARPETS OF FLOWERS

In all the northern part of the island, there is evidence of a remarkable change in the methods of business management as well as modern agricultural methods. Greenhouses, for example, appear more and more everywhere on the island: they facilitate the growing of new agricultural products, thus ensuring the producer a better annual income and consequently a higher standard of living.

Leaving Tacoronte behind, we come to El Sauzal and from there to La Matanza and Victoria de Acentejo, two historical places where the Guanches and the Spaniards clashed in dramatic battles, and where the slaughter assumed enormous proportions. Today these places are part of the agricultural zone: they are small communities developing at a fairly good rhythm and are integrated into the rosary of villages and cities that line the old winding road, a road much less in use nowadays since the building of the new and and modern highway.

Reaching Santa Ursula, we arrive at the entrance to the most important tourist zone of the Canarian Archipelago, where we notice the overwhelming profusion of flowers and an ideal climate in the proximity of the ocean.

Reaching Orotava, we find ourselves in the region that is most propitious for the growth of the vine. It is worth while lingering a few hours in this old aristocratic town; the more so because it is strongly linked with the past of Tenerife, as is evident from its old mansions and houses with their polished wooden balconies of Canarian pine; delightful patios emitting the intoxicating scent of colourful flowers and vast quantities of green plants.

Everything in Orotava, whether the ancient mansions or the narrow streets with their beautiful old trees, carry an atmosphere of part grandeur...

CARPETS OF FLOWERS

27

The town is situated in the Valley of La Orotava, and it was on beholding the unique panorama of this immense valley, that the German naturalist Humboldt went down on his knees to praise its solitary beauty. For there are but few places in the world where one can overlook a valley of such immensity and splendour and offering all the contrasts nature can provide. In the background the majestic outlines of the gigantic Teide, the highest mountain of Spain, set off gloriously against the blue sky. Below the forest of pines stand cypresses, the green fields dotted here and there with palm trees, their leaves gently waying in the wind. Still further below come the vast zones of banana plantations and the ocean extending to the horizon: this immense ocean alive and moving, on some days with its foam-crowned waves beating against

BOTANICAL GARDENS

the hard black rocks, on others calm and quiet with the small waves dying in a gentle murmur on the small beaches, where foreigners who have escaped the hard European winter lie basking in the sun.

Orotava is a town of artisans. This is evident from the artwork of the beautifully carved balconies, or of the striking doors and windows in **tea** wood. The people of Orotava have become masters in the art of

PLAYA DE MARTIANEZ

working the wood. It is a tradition which continues to be kept up and finds its climax in the annual Exhibition of Handicraft Furniture, on which occasion the best carpenters compete to demonstrate the skill of their handicraft. The reputation of their art has gone beyond the frontiers of the islands.

The people of Orotava are apparently endowed with particular artistic gifts as revealed on the day of celebration of Corpus Christi.

During this festival the squares and streets of the town are covered with ephemeral flower carpets for the passing of the Procession. The largest and most extraordinary carpet is usually spread out on the Plaza del Ayuntamiento. It is the master-piece of an art that is almost unique, for the natural carpet covering the square is an elaborate combination of the various colorful lava stones from the volcanic region of Las Cañadas; other carpets are made with hundreds of thousands of flower petals that

PARTIAL VIEW OF PUERTO DE LA CRUZ

trace symbolic pictures of angels, animals or biblical scenes. Every year thousands of people flock to La Orotava to admire these carpets and take a closer look at this fascinating artwork. The streets, too, are resplendent with magnificent flower arrangements. No wonder that during the festival of Corpus Christi the place becomes an artistic and religious centre and that the sight of this miraculous art remains forever imprinted in the memory of those who have witnessed it.

35

This tradition, born in Orotava, has in time extended to other towns and villages in the Canaries, but nowhere does it reach a zenith as in Orotava.

Ever since the last century Puerto de la Cruz has been a favourite holiday resort for foreigners, though during pre-war years the guests were mainly the English who spent the winter months in the Canaries, in order to escape the cold and misty winter of their own country. It was a quiet, distinguished and rather conservative clientele who filled the first few hotels. But even at that time it was already a favourite resort

SWIMMING POOLS

for well-known personalities of political, social and intellectual circles. A truly different atmosphere pervaded Puerto at that time, and the traditional afternoon tea on the terraces and in the lobbies of the old hotels gave the place a typical English atmosphere.

Puerto de la Cruz, once the principal port of the Valley of La Orotava, has now detached itself from the municipal community and has become an independent community.

The rapid development of Puerto is due to several facts. Due to travel promo-

SWIMMING POOLS

tions, the exellent climate has become known all over the world, and the easy travelling facilities of modern times enable thousands of foreigners to take advantage of it. Last but not least the beauty of its luxurious and exotic vegetation delights every visitor and lures him back year after year. The most impressive example of this luxuriant vegetation are the Botanical Gardens which were founded in this zone. Situated halfway between Orotava and Puerto de la Cruz, it is a miniature virgin forest of miraculous beauty, where hundress of tropical species from all over the world are to be found.

Due to these fascinating surroundings and to its gentle climate, the miracle of the development of Puerto de la Cruz has come about. From a small harbour it developed in the shortest of times into the main tourist centre of the island and the skyscrapers of its huge modern apartment houses and hotels resemble the skyline of large modern cities.

Modern edifices have replaced old farmhouses, fincas, agricultural land and banana plantations. Forgotten are the times when Puerto was merely an embarkation port and the only outlet for the agricultural produced of Orotava. The Puerto of today is a conglomeration of modern hotels, cafeterias, restaurants, night clubs, luxury stores, boutiques, travel agencies, banks and souvenir shops, along the various streets and promenades.

The whole picture of Puerto is changing. Narrow old streets are being turned into broad avenues, crowded in high season by promenading tourists. New technical systems have been developed to build arti-

BIRD'S EYE VIEW OF SAN TELMO

VIEW OF SAN TELMO

ficial swimming pools into the hard, rocky coastline. In short, no effort is being spared to offer holiday-makers every possible comfort and to endeavour to make their stay unforgettable.

Every year Puerto is invaded by more tourists from around the world. But though Puerto is the holiday resort par excellence, yet a great part of the population consists of working people such as architects, technicians, managers, developers, hotel employees, clerks shopkeepers etc...

In a way, the town is really divided into the modern Puerto with its ultra-modern buildings and hotels and the old town with its narrow streets which still seem to belong to the native population. But perhaps it is this contrast between old and new which gives Puerto de la Cruz a distinct and special character, attractive to the visitor.

Puerto de la Cruz is a new city. Much has been done to develop tourism and many more projects are planned to comply with the demands of our guests from abroad. Today these guests are mainly Germans.

PUERTO DE LA CRUZ

42

In fact they represent by far the largest percentage of visitors, followed by Swedes, Norwegians, Belgians, French, Dutch and English… From all parts of the world thousands of men and women come to Puerto de la Cruz to seek relaxation far from the hectic life in Europe. On our island of Eternal Spring, they come to find the sunshine and mild winters which the old continent lacks.

The promoters of Puerto de la Cruz have truly exerted themselves in the years past, and the changes brought about in recent years must appear remarkable to any tourist who knew Puerto some years ago, and finds himself confronted today with an ultra-modern cosmopolitan city. Tea-time at definite hours in quiet old hotels has become a somewhat nostalgic remembrance of days gone by.

SWIMMING POOL IN A TOURIST CENTRE

Let us therefore rate at its true value the efforts of the various technicians, architects, specialists, and all the people who have contributed to construct the various buildings, who have made it possible to build new roads and modernize Puerto, and to whose knowledge and devotion we owe this miraculous result. For these people have made Puerto de la Cruz a dominant tourist town, and have simultaneously succeeded in preserving its lively historical past amidst modern splendour. It is thanks

PART OF LA ROMANTICA ON THE NORTH COAST

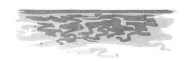

to these people that the small harbour of Puerto has extended far beyond the rural limits... Apartment houses and hotels not only border the coast by the sea, but are gradually extending up to the slopes of the hills.

The change is striking and cannot be overlooked. Rural life has given way to the activity of a bustling town, and productive farming is being replaced by the layout of gardens and parks.

BAYS ON THE NORTH COAST

Driving northwards, we reach the village of Los Realejos in the Valley of Orotava. This community was the last stronghold of Guanche resistance before surrendering to the Spanish conqueror Fernández de Lugo and submitting themselves as vassals of the Catholic kings. A church dedicated to Santiago was built in Realejo Alto, making it the first parish where the Guanche chieftains were baptised.

The road continues towards San Juan de la Rambla and La Guancha, and from there on to Icod de los Vinos, which town owes its name to the prodigious growth of its vineyards. It is situated in a particularly fertile and prosperous region amongst green fields, vineyards and banana plantations. The small bays, with beaches of black

ICOD DE LOS VINOS

sand, were once an ideal refuge for fishing boats, but today the tourists have taken possession of them.

Icod de los Vinos prides itself on having the oldest tree on the island, the Drago Millenario, a special point of attraction for visitors. One would almost say it is indeed the symbol of Icod, this enormous tree with its thick rough trunk from which grow pointed sabre-like green leaves. It is supposed to be almost 3,000 years old, and it is said that the red sap, the mysterious dragon blood, was used in the embalming of the Guanche kings.

Climbing up the narrow streets of Icod, we come across an ancient convent, old houses and the church with its tower, and

DRAGON-TREE IN ICOD DE LOS VINOS

in the background the constant presence of the dominant Teide.

From Icod downwards we reach Garachico. From this point Los Silos and Buenavista can be reached as well as Punta de Teno, where a lighthouse throws its familiar searchlight beams through the darkness of the night. This whole region from Icod de los Vinos is called «the lower island».

But before reaching Garachico, we have the well known playa of San Marcos ensconced under a wall of lava, where tourism has developed strongly. Its sunny beach of black volcanic sand offers all necessary facilities, and the colourful fishing boats drawn on to the beach render it a most picturesque sight.

Whoever wishes to know the island of Tenerife thoroughly, should not merely drive along the coastline, but into the interior to explore its heights, valleys and plains.

Whether in winter or summer, radiant sunshine or glittering snow, on clear autumn days or during springtime, it is a must for every tourist to drive up to the Teide.

Many impressive sights await the visitor to the volcanic area from the midst of which

PANORAMIC VIEW OF THE SAN MARCOS BEACH

TYPICAL RUSTIC HOUSE (FARM = HOUSE)

arises Teide. In this region the earth's surface has suffered a terrific upheaval by the natural force of volcanic eruptions, and the broken surface reveals many strata of different hued stones and rocks forced up from below ground level.

One drives slowly up from the north, passing white villas and farmhouses. Higher up we travel through magnificent pine forests, and almost always and everywhere one can get a glimpse of the sea below.

On reaching the heights at the foot of the Teide, one inhales deeply the rarified air and surveys the impressive sight of this lunar scenery called Las Cañadas, which stuns most people to silence.

GARACHICO

MONTE DE LA ESPERANZA AND TEIDE

It is scenery foreign to most visitors, almost as though they have been transported to another planet. A tormented and devastated zone thousand year old scars due to hot liquid lava from erupting volcanoss that transformed the immense plain into a fantastic landscape. Colossal geological scars, overwhelming in the revelation of the terrific forces of nature.

TEIDE NEVADO

Then the miracle of life: gorse growing here and there, the colourful and rare taji-nastes blooming in the midst of this dead plain, and here and there among the topaz and tourmaline, gleaming masses of rocks, or the wonder of a solitary pine tree.

The ascent to the summit of the Teide is highly recommended. Part of the road can be travelled on mule-back, at least until the mountain shelter. There one should

NATURE'S WHIM

spend the night and start the further ascent on foot at dawn. It takes about an hour and a half to climb to the peak and to reach the vast crater where the exudation of sulphurous fumes reminds us that the fire monster is not yet dead; it is simply lying dormant.

The view covers the whole of the archipelago, all seven islands, and as a basis the island of Tenerife from the midst of which arises the majestic, domineering Teide. In the misty light of dawn, the islands around resemble ships floating in the ocean. One almost imagines that one can perceive San Borondon, that mythological piece of land which many islanders pretend to have seen arise from the sea.

Is this the mythical Atlantis?

Perhaps... Or at least we would like to believe so.

Today a funicular railway takes tourists up to the peak. Thanks to modern technique, it is now possible for older or weaker people to be transported to the top of the Teide, and to witness this magnificent spectacle. However, any tourist who can make the ascent by foot is advised to do so. It is truly worthwhile.

But all this immense and fascinating area representing the Parque Nacional de Las Cañadas del Teide, should not receive just a cursory glance. One should understand it, contemplate it, feel it. For there is much to ponder about and more to discover than the eye can see. For in the midst of this dead sea of stones and rocks which the angry, rumbling fire-monster once created, the miracle of life remains triumphant. Amidst death and devastation there miraculously grows the legendary violet of the Teide, which has almost become a myth, yet is there to be seen by only a few visitors who have the good fortune to find it. The violet is reality, likewise the solitary hawk circling over the peak, and the bee that

EL PORTILLO

57

THE PARADOR DE TURISMO

builds its honeycomb there. Yet how many fail to notice all these miracles: for it is given to only a few to really see and observe the wonders of nature around us.

Neither could the lava stop the growth of the pine trees. They stand there among the dark stone masses, gently swaying in the breeze. Trees that took shape and form, grew strong and healthy, living for hundreds of years in their own simple environment; they do not even need fresh water from the springs, for the dew that falls on damp nights irrigates the soil on which they stand.

The pine trees live scattered in those

heights, solitary, part of the silence, companions of the stones, the snow and the wind. Nothing could stop the beginning of this life, the birth of the first seeds. It was as though they were meant to become the permanent sentinals of the peaks, with only the wind as playing companion.

Amidst this lunar landscape we find extraordinary and curious rock formations, and feel the wind that for century after century has chiselled the stones to new forms. It is hard to believe, standing in this place, that just below there exists the idyllic

THE ROQUE «CINCHADO»

northern part of the island, fertile and green, with its pastures, houses and hotels, towns and holiday resorts. Unbelievable also that only a few miles from Las Cañadas people cultivate fields and orchards. For on Las Cañadas everything seems bare and lifeless, and one has to linger here in order that one has time to appreciate the whims and wonders of nature.

Driving southwards we come to Vilaflor, one of the most picturesque villages of the island. Vilaflor, with its red tiled roofs,

CABLE CAR UP TO THE TEIDE

IN THE CRATER OF THE TEIDE

is the true expression of popular architecture of times past, and holds a special enchantment. The whole of the village is redolent with the scent of the surrounding pine trees. It is the highest situated village of the whole archipelago and is noted for its salubrious climate.

Visitors stopping at Vilaflor should sample a glass of their white wine: an excellent wine to accompany the fine goat cheese that is made and sold there. Vilaflor has remained one of the most typical places

«TAJINASTES» IN BLOOM AT THE FOOT OF THE TEIDE

on the island and one of the few villages that have remained untouched by modern technique, by modern buildings or tourism. It is a charming village with flowers blooming everywhere on the wayside and with houses that have well kept little patios and gardens.

Vilaflor represents serene rural peace in the truest sense of the word — a silent and peaceful little village embedded among magnificent pine woods.

Until a few years ago, it was difficult to reach the South. The journey over Las Cañadas on the narrow winding roads took several hours, and due to ravines by the wayside, danger threatened on many bends.

However, a new life is emerging for the South since the opening of the new modern highway in 1971, which has considerably hastened the development of the southern part of the island.

The broad and modern autopista now allows rapid communication between Santa Cruz and the South. This fast access to the sunny side of the island has resulted in tourist development all along the coastline. Due to the magnificent motorway, new holiday resorts are being built along the

STRANGE LAVA AND STONE FORMATIONS

A CHEERFUL DETAIL IN THE SOLITARY HEIGHTS

seafront and agricultural progress equally benifits from this facility: transportation is simplified and agriculture is developing on modern lines. Greenhouses are being erected in the South, expediting the growth

VIEW OF THE MOUNTAIN TOP

of new species of flowers, plants and vege-
tables. Until recently tomatoes and potatoes
were the main wealth-producing crops of
the southern region, but today various addi-
tional agricultural products have assumed
considerable importance.

Nevertheless, it appears that tourism
will, in the future, become the foremost
industry of the South. As soon as the new
motorway was open, many urbanizations

67

LUNAR LANDSCAPE

CASA FORESTAL AND TAJINASTES

69

PEACEFUL CORNER AT VILAFLOR

were built and developed along the coastline; for example, the picturesque urbanization Tabaiba, or Las Caletillas with its modern hotels and its lovely beach of black lava sand. Both these urbanizations are situated in a good climatic zone, and have the advantage of being situated close to the capital.

OUT IN THE COUNTRY

Three kilometres further on, we have the village of Candelaria with its impressive Basílica of Nuestra Señora de Candelaria, the Patron Saint of the Canary Archipelago. The feast of the Virgin of Candelaria is in August, and during that time pilgrims from all over the world come to pray to the little dark Virgin, whose statue, so the legend goes, was once apon a time washed ashore on to the beach of Tenerife.

PANORAMA OF THE SOUTH COAST

Soon we reach Güímar, situated in the fertile valley of Güímar; a valley that in its immensity appears almost like the pendant of the valley of La Orotava. The beach, well sheltered from the winds, is always crowded on Sundays.

Driving on, the visitor passes beautiful bays and magnificent scenery of dark cliffs falling steeply into the water. It is really a

LAS CALETILLAS

LAS CALETILLAS

great experience to drive along this motorway from which one has a continuous view of the ocean.

Vast urbanizations offering every comfort and variety of recreation facilities are being situated more towards the South. Visitors from all over the world fly to Tenerife all the year through, to benefit from the excellent climate and permanent sunshine. They come to spend their holidays here, and often decide to make this their place of retirement, resulting in the rapid growth of residential quarters, bungalows and apartment houses.

CANDELARIA — AND VIEW OF THE BASILICA

From Poris to Los Abrigos, from picturesque Chayofa to Médano, from Los Cris-
tianos to Playa Las Américas, not forgetting
the Costa del Silencio, the whole South is
developing into an immense modern holiday
area. A new airport being planned in the
South, a colossal project in the vicinity of
El Médano, will greatly enhance the prestige
and importance of the South.

THE ROCKS OF FASNIA

EL PORIS BEACH

Underwater fishing is very popular here, as well as many other types of aquatic sport. Motorboats can be hired for underwater fishing or deep sea fishing, and holidaymakers usually return from these expeditions with quite impressive catches.

There are many points of interest in the South, such as Granadilla, considered the capital of the South, and the picturesque

CHAYOFA

villages of San Miguel, Guía de Isora, Arona and Adeje.

Most of these villages are situated in fertile agricultural zones, for although a visitor's general impression might probably be that everything centres around the development of tourism, yet it is still agriculture on which the islander bases his life. Modern machines are lacking, and farmers still use rudimentary implements for working the land, so that the picturesque sight of a camel used for ploughing the field is a familiar,

EL MEDANO BEACH

TEN-BEL

though rare sight. But the difficulty of fertilising the dry, barren land of the South, has been greatly modified in the past by various water channels that facilitate the irrigation of agricultural zones; this results is higher rentability and more rational work.

But the tourist industry, the industry without a chimney as we call it, is of significant importance. True, there is nothing as yet to compare with Puerto de la Cruz, but there is no limit to the possibilities of the South.

SWIMMING-POOL OF TEN-BEL (LA BALLENA)

Tenerife is a miniature continent. The visitor who has known the rich, green North, visited the volcanic lunar landscapes on Las Cañadas, taken walks through the pine forests or roamed the countryside, will no doubt realize how strikingly different is every part of the island. Tenerife is truly

SWIMMING-POOL OF TEN-BEL (LA BALLENA)

82

the world in a nutshell. It has unique prodigies of nature, for example, the Barranco del Infierno (the Devil's Ravine) in Adeje. This is a deep and immense ravine wherein one can walk for hours. No sunrays ever penetrate the very depths of this ravine, and yet it is a miraculous vegetative and geological world which is encountered down there.

After Adeje we continue to drive on the motorway towards the south-east of the island. With the exception of a few zones, vegetation is scanty, the land hot, dry and arid. But the skies here are forever cloudless and blue, and the rugged coastline holds a special power of attraction.

TEN-BEL COSTA DEL SILENCIO

As we approach the Acantilados, we can see from the motorway one of the most charming bays and beaches of the whole South: namely the Playa de La Arena in Puerto de Santiago. Nearby we have one of the most fascinating and impressive sights: the magnificent cliffs of El Acantilado falling vertically to the sea. Nowhere does the ocean seem so clear and limpid, or of such turquise colour. Here the water is rich in fish and day by day the fishermen return with their boats laden with their precious silver catch.

E BARRANCO DEL INFIERNO

El Acantilado of Los Gigantes has developed recently into a tourist centre of some importance. Bungalows and apartment houses are gradually being built around the modern and beautiful hotel of Los Gigantes. There is no doubt that few places on the island can compare with this idyllic spot. It is again a different world, a different scenery, and justifies the saying that Tenerife is more a myth than a reallity.

LA ARENA BEACH IN PUERTO DE SANTIAGO

EL ACANTILADO DE LOS GIGANTES

The inhabitants of Tenerife are a gay and carefree people. They like to celebrate feasts and are fond of music. There actually exists a typical Canarian music, which is simultaneously vivid and nostalgic. The Canarians like to sign, and many of them play the guitar or timple, the latter being the typical small Canarian guitar. The natives have preserved successfully the Canarian folklore, and visitors will frequently be able to see the Canarians perform such typical dances as the folias, isas, malagueñas and others, either at festivities or as a tourist attraction.

EL ACANTILADO DE LOS GIGANTES

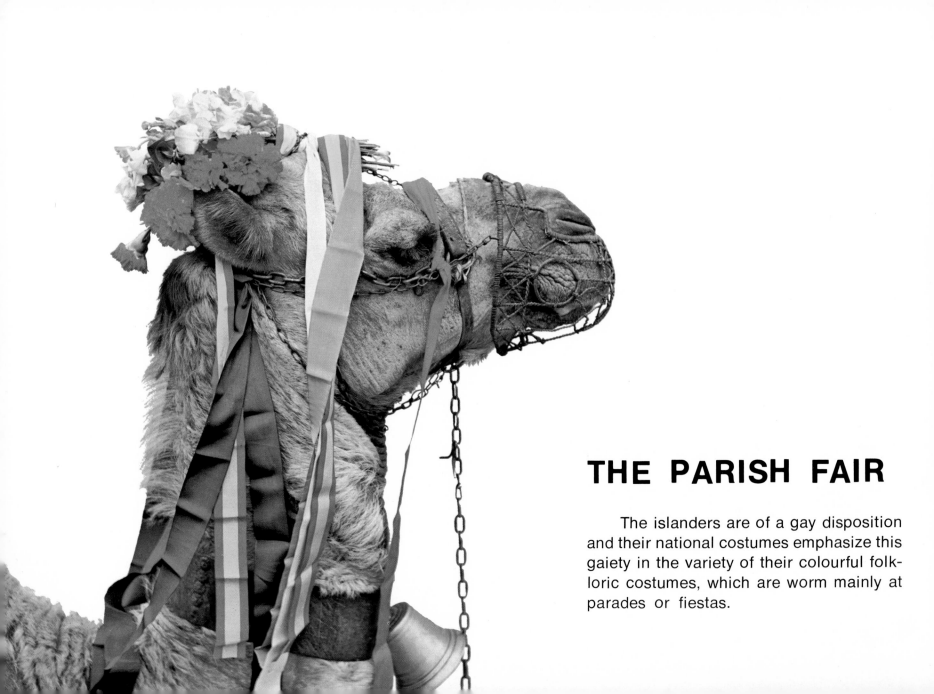

THE PARISH FAIR

The islanders are of a gay disposition and their national costumes emphasize this gaiety in the variety of their colourful folk-loric costumes, which are worm mainly at parades or fiestas.

The village inn is the gastronomic centre of the fiesta. In the black furnace or on an open grill, spicy pigs or rabbits are prepared, filling the air with a delicious aroma. The meat is usually served with «papas arrugadas», i.e. potatoes boiled in their skin, accompanied by salsa mojo, a strongly seasoned, typically Canarian sauce. When a fiesta or celebration takes place in the North of the island, red wine will probably accompany the food, while the Southerner prefers white wine. Visitors can photograph many a beautiful picture at these colourful gay fiestas, in which even camels sometimes participate.

FOLKLORIC GROUP

The island of Tenerife is a gay island with a slightly melancholic note, for the Canarians represent a mixture of various inheritances and tendencies. Their character reveals the pride and vivacity of the Spaniards combined with the nostalgic temperament of their noble ancestors, the Guanches. Immigrants from South America have also influenced Canarian music and dances.

Tenerife with its characteristic people and their folklore, with its history and legends, its unique nature and climate, its joy of living and hospitality, its sun and blue sky, is a Fortunate Island indeed. For all these beauties and joys combined tend to make the island of Tenerife a true paradise on earth.

A CAMEL PARTICIPATING AT THE FIESTA